MIND HACKING

Train Your Brain to Automatically Make Better Decisions, Stop Racing Thoughts and Enhance Your Quality of Life

Noah Grayton

Legal & Disclaimer

The information contained in this book and its contents is not designed to replace or take the place of any form of medical or professional advice; and is not meant to replace the need for independent medical, financial, legal or other professional advice or services, as may be required. The content and information in this book has been provided for educational and entertainment purposes only.

The content and information contained in this book has been compiled from sources deemed reliable, and it is accurate to the best of the Author's knowledge, information and belief. However, the Author cannot guarantee its accuracy and validity and cannot be held liable for any errors and/or omissions. Further, changes are periodically made to this book as and when needed. Where appropriate and/or necessary, you must consult a professional (including but not limited to your doctor, attorney, financial advisor or such other professional advisor) before using any of the suggested remedies, techniques, or information in this book.

Upon using the contents and information contained in this book, you agree to hold harmless the Author from and against any damages, costs, and expenses, including any legal fees potentially resulting from the application of any of the information provided by this book. This disclaimer applies to any loss, damages or injury caused by the use and application, whether directly or indirectly, of any advice or information presented, whether for breach of contract, tort, negligence, personal injury, criminal intent, or under any other cause of action.

You agree to accept all risks of using the information presented inside this book.

You agree that by continuing to read this book, where appropriate and/or necessary, you shall consult a professional (including but not limited to your doctor, attorney, or financial advisor or such other advisor as needed) before using any of the suggested remedies, techniques, or information in this book.

Table of Contents

Introduction to Mind Hacking

The mind is a powerful tool, capable of great feats of logic and imagination of which the applications are almost endless. We've all read accounts of people achieving great improbable feats in business, life and arts through the use of their minds.

We don't promise anything on that level but we do have a lot to offer here in regards to your well-being, determination, charisma and for "hacking" your overall outlook to maximize your potential in whatever life endeavors you are in right now. As an added bonus, the techniques here can be practiced immediately and won't require you to spend a lifetime studying. So, why not make the most of what your mind can do right now? Let's discuss some items that are quick, super simple, easy and the most beneficial to you and your mindset.

1. **Take regular breaks** - When working on projects at home, there is nothing wrong with taking regular breaks as long as you don't overdo it. Work an hour or two and then read for 10 to 15 minutes or enjoy a snack and a coffee. Above all, LET YOURSELF ENJOY IT. Don't rush. Taking this mindset can allow you to turn what might be a frustrating 5 or 6-hour workday and turn it into an incredibly productive 8 to 10 hour one. This works for a large and small project but most

especially for the large ones, as the regular breaks encourage you to think more in terms of productivity rather than reminding yourself that you are working.

2. **Break big problems down into smaller, manageable ones** - This is good for large projects. Take a piece of paper or open up Notepad on your trusted PC and write down your goal. Then next, in outline fashion, break this goal down into smaller, quickly manageable goals. Use this like a checklist and that way, rather than thinking your goal is too big, you can see it for what it actually is, a number of manageable steps in the direction of your desired outcome.

3. **De-clutter (or re-clutter) your work environment** - Some of us like our desks messy but generally, even among those, we find ourselves working more efficiently in an organized work environment. If you really DO enjoy the clutter, why not give it a 're-clutter' so that the only clutter present is related to the work at hand. This way the room still feels comfortable to you but it's a functional-yet-messy comfortable. Whichever you prefer and what makes you the most productive is best but we do recommend that you try de-cluttering, even if you are the messy type. You might find that you like it.

4. **Read for clearing your mind** - While television and Youtube are a great distraction, if you are working on something and really want to isolate yourself from the world outside for your break, consider grabbing a cup of coffee and

reading for the duration it takes you to drink it (don't abuse that, you know who you are!). Reading is particularly immersive in its own manner and unlike those forms of media you might just access on your PC, curling up with a book from an author you like can help to give you that form of isolation most conducive to getting your mind refreshed and ready to go. Best of all, books are quite portable (E-books even more so, there's nothing like having an entire library in your bag). Consider this option for optimal mind-cleansing between those diligent work periods, you'll be happy that you did.

5. **Compete** - Some of you may not agree with this one but give us a moment. As a species, we have always been quite competitive, and healthy competition can bring out the best in us. We aren't saying that every day at work you should try to one-up Joe or Jan in the next cubicle at absolutely everything; rather that, when you are working with others in your same line of work, a little 'secret competition' mindset can give you an edge that being humble just isn't going to match. Again, we stress, don't overdo it, but also don't overlook the advantages of being competitive in the workplace. It helps your pride and it can help when it's time to ask for that raise.

6. **Journal completed goals** - If you are very goal oriented, a nice mental boost can be had by keeping a journal for yourself and documenting dates and particular goals achieved. These don't have to be monumental. 'Worked out 3 times this week'

or 'Drank 5 less sodas this week/1500 less calories, hooray!' are a couple of fine examples. The reasoning behind this is so that you can open it every now and again and see that you are accomplishing things all the time. Start with small goals and don't forget to list some big ones that you've accomplished before the journal came into play. This exercise can give you a physical item that you can keep at home or throw in your bag for an instant morale boost.

7. **Mnemonic devices** - There are a number of examples of these available on the web. Mnemonic devices are tricks for helping you to remember important things. For instance, one method is rhyming. You want to remember a co-worker's name. His name is Joe. Think about some personal characteristic that they have. 'His name is Joe and he talks slow, his name I know, oh Joe Joe Joe.' It sounds silly but it's quite effective and only one example. Try it or check out a few others online, they are useful Mindset Hacks that everyone can use and enjoy.

8. **Resist procrastination at dangerous times** - Specifically the planning phases and when completing a project. These are particularly vulnerable. For the former we like to think 'I'm brainstorming' because we don't want to sit down and do the outline right away. This leads to issues that perhaps miss being identified because the task was put off. As far as when nearing project completion is concerned, one needs to worry about telling themselves 'eh, it's almost done, I can go

out tonight' or worse, 'I can go ahead and take on that next project now..' Combat procrastination with scheduled work periods that you do not deviate from until the project is complete. Don't sabotage your chances at earning larger projects and larger benefits!

9. **Reward yourself quarterly** - There is nothing wrong with rewarding yourself. You can even set it to work with your goal journal by starting an extra bank account and putting a little bit into savings every time you achieve a particular goal. Resist the urge to touch it (thus, the second account) until the end of the yearly quarter. Then use what you have saved to get something you like. Perhaps some items you collect. Maybe a projector if you are a movie buff. It doesn't have to be elaborate or expensive but don't be afraid to splurge on what you've put aside as a reward for meeting your goals. A little incentive can lead to a more productive overall lifestyle and really boost morale.

10. **Powernaps** - 15 to 30-minute naps, or 'Powernaps' as they are most well-known, can be a great way to get your energy levels back in gear when you feel them flagging. Many businesses have recognized this and actually have napping rooms onsite. If your workplace does not and if your manager approves, simply setting a timer and laying your head on your desk will suffice in most cases. While it sounds like a gimmick, many well-known people in history have utilized this technique

to great effect, including Winston Churchill, Salvador Dali, and Albert Einstein!

11. **Add personal items to your work cubicle** - Personalizing your workspace has been shown to improve productivity. It is generally thought that this performance increase is brought on by the fact that we have symbolically 'made this space our own' or in cases of cohabitation with a spouse or loved one, oddly enough the work cubicle can end up being one of the most personalized spaces that we actually have. In either case, give yourself a mental boost by personalizing your space. You are not a number, but a powerful individual. Take advantage of this mind hack so that you can show everyone that this is the case.

12. **Charisma hack** - Studies have shown that most people appreciate a certain amount of eye contact on initial meetings and that this can have a large effect as to whether or not they like you. A quick way to ensure that you are 'hedging your bets' and getting the proper amount of eye contact is to take a moment to determine someone's eye color when you are introduced. This is quick and can help you to take advantage of this psychological mind hack.

13. **The Churchill** - Everyone knows Winston Churchill. One of the things that he was famous for was his razor wit but what you may not know is that most of his responses were planned in advance. You see, Winston suffered from a speech

impediment in his youth that led him to a habit of rehearsing very carefully what he would say. This habit would continue later in life when the speech impediment was no longer a problem. While you cannot predict everything you will need to say the next day, if you know there is a particular meeting coming and there are things that you wish to say, rehearse them! If you know there will be particular arguments, rehearse your rebuttals. Planning ahead can ensure that you go into meetings and the general workplace with confidence and co-workers will raise their estimations of your character. Consider a little preplanning and see what it can do for you!

14. **Get people to talk about themselves** - One social mind hack that you can use is simple. When meeting new people, get them to talk about themselves. Everyone, to an extent, enjoys talking about themselves, and this will often put them in a mindset to view you favorably. At the very least, you will learn more information about the individual, so what is there to lose? Try this psychological mind hack for yourself if you have a little trouble socializing sometimes. You'll be glad that you did!

15. **Consolidation learning** - This one is quite interesting. A study at Harvard showed that large amounts of information could actually be absorbed by a 24-hour study period followed by a deep sleep. Apparently, the science behind this is that your brain acquires information through 3 methods: acquisition,

consolidation, and recall. Consolidation is the one that we are interested in. What happens is that during sleep, your brain attempts to process all of the data that it 'skimmed over' during the day. By providing nothing but information, the brain is left with no choice but to process as much of this batch as possible. While this is certainly not something one could do many times during the week, it is a mind hack with some serious potential.

16. **The Ben Franklin Effect** - There is a famous story about how Ben Franklin turned the ire of a Pennsylvania legislator into a friendship that lasted for the rest of the legislator's days. How did he do it? This is the interesting bit. He asked him for a favor. Franklin had learned that the legislator had a particularly rare book in his library and so he wrote a letter asking the man if he could borrow this book for a few days. Franklin returned the book with a letter thanking him profusely for the loan of this book and a funny thing happened. The next time the men met, the ire was gone, and he talked to Franklin for the first time. The theory behind this is that when someone performs a favor for us then a part of their brain convinces them 'hey, I did a favor for this person, I must like them.' Do a google search on this phenomenon and see what you think. This might be a useful mind hack for you as well!

17. **Bubble-Gum boost** - Need a quick pick-me-up when you are about to take a test and need to recall something? Try a little bubble gum. A study involving 224 undergraduates at the

St. Lawrence University found that students chewing gum while taking their tests produced scores that were significantly higher than those who didn't. Keep some handy in your pocket, you never know when this mind hack might be useful!

18. **Job interview with an old friend** - Don't you hate going to job interviews? They can be quite intimidating, with strangers asking us personal and trick questions that sometimes require thinking outside of the box to answer properly. One trick that you can use to help alleviate the stress from this experience is to pretend that the interviewer or interviewers are old friends that you haven't seen in many years. Put yourself in this mindset and you will find that you can answer their questions with a more casual confidence and who knows, perhaps you'll get that new job! Give this one a try at your next interview and let this mind hack work for you!

19. **Take control with selective choices** - When it seems that you have no choice in a situation, often the inverse is true. There are choices but they are not necessarily good ones. While it is unpleasant, you need to realize that this is going to be the case sometimes. What empowers you is how you deal with it. Take the emotion from the situation and remove the feeling of helplessness by breaking down your options and simply asking yourself 'Will I choose option a, b, or c?.' Teaching yourself to react calmly and weigh your available options anyway, even when there are nothing but bad choices, are a very, very useful

mind hack. If it helps, pretend that you are a machine making the decision or Mr. Spock from the old Star Trek television series. Take out the emotion and give it some logic.

20. **Stress mirrors courage** - We've saved one of the best for last. Did you know that the reactions that your body feels to stress, such as elevated heartbeat, change in breathing patterns, a rise in adrenaline... are the same responses that your body has during acts of courage? When you start getting these feelings, focus on viewing the stress as a challenge, rather than a threat. This is called 'Cognitive reframing' and it can be quite useful if you practice it. The next time you find yourself under heavy stress then give it a whirl. Hack your mindset by telling yourself that this is a challenge and that your body is getting you ready to plow right through it. This hack is definitely worth keeping.

Take some time to practice the hacks we've just provided and we are certain that you will see results quickly, if not immediately. Give the more complicated ones a week or two to gauge your results and if you truly want to take a scientific approach to it, create a journal where you note which techniques that you are trying and document the results on a day by day basis. You'll appreciate the results of your hard work! We'll proceed next to a chapter that is also quite useful. In Chapter 4: Goal Achievement Hacks, we will discuss ways that you hack your mindset to better flush out and achieve your goals, as well as a number of ways to keep yourself productive and on-track. If you are ready, let's go there together and see what you can do about those goals of yours!

Chapter 1: Welcome the Unexpected

Now that you understand the importance of setting reasonable but challenging small targets in your quest for success, it's time to talk about your lack of control in achieving your goals.

That's right: you don't have ultimate control over what happens to you on the outside. No matter how well you plan, how many post-it notes you have around your work station, how many journals full of objectives and your progress towards them, life will still throw you some curveballs. There will be unexpected twists to your story, as there are for everyone. The question is: how will you respond these random occurrences, some of which could threaten your mental stability if you are already turning negative.

That's what this chapter will deal with as you welcome the unknown, a key part of Mind Hacking.

There are several ways to keep your cool and embrace the unanticipated events that might seem to threaten to derail you, but can actually make you a stronger and better person:

- No matter how bad it might seem in the moment when you are hit with a surprise, there is always tomorrow. Keep the jolt that you just received in perspective; time will not stop with this bad news, such as a job loss, business loss or a relationship breakup. Tomorrow will come, and you can resume your march towards success as the pain of this new circumstance diminishes and you renew your focus. As has been stated earlier, don't begin to feel sorry for yourself when bad news comes. **Accept the present** as it is with the **intention** to change it as fast as possible, with whatever resources you have available in the moment. Staying present with intention is the key, plus whatever small actions you can take to move forward.

- Ask yourself what you can learn from this unexpected development. View these jarring moments as teachers. What is the lesson to draw from the death of a loved one? What did that person teach you? What would that person want you to do as you proceed to build a great life and career? This is a fantastic mind- set, rather than simply dwelling in the emotional dumps and not seeing any light at all. Your first question when the boss tells you that staff cutbacks have included you should be: *What can I to learn from this?*

- If the unexpected is negative, as it often is, remember that the most successful people in the world talk about how they learned more from failure than success. Failure is often necessary for success. Abraham Lincoln lost many elections before becoming president; Thomas Edison had hundreds of failed experiments before he invented the light bulb. The list goes on and on, and many of these great people will tell you that failure was a wonderful teacher. View the unexpected not as a roadblock, but as a wise instructor. That way, you can embrace your lack of control, not fret about it. People who have achieved greatness did not let failure shatter their self-image. They kept all failures separate from their belief in themselves, which never wavered. This is a key concept in Mind Hacking.

- Realize that of all the elements of life that you can't control, one element that you can control is your thoughts and response. That's an old saying that we don't always want to hear, but it has lasted because it's true. Nothing, no one can rob you of a positive attitude as you seek greatness. Many successful entrepreneurs testify of having a positive outlook. They refuse to let the unexpected stop them from achieving their goals. They have the perspective that calls to mind the maxim: if the door is closed, look for an open window. The unexpected can often mean a closed door. Step back, absorb this reality, then determine to either push harder on the door or look for a window. That's what successful people do, rather than sit in the hallway and mourn, convinced that the world is against them or that they are not worthy of open doors.

- Frame the unexpected as a challenge to keep you stimulated. If you are going to see true change in your life and career, you are going to have to have to get more intense. That's one reason why smaller targets are best; when you don't reach them, it's easy to pick yourself up, dust yourself off, and try again. Anyone who wants to change his or her life is going to have to appreciate challenge, not want the easy way out. Part of Mind Hacking is loving a challenge, not an assumption that life is always easy.

- As you greet the unexpected as a friend, not an enemy, you look at it as a golden opportunity to prove yourself and to meet a new challenge. As you do this repeatedly, you quickly develop a reservoir of past victories over hurdles. When you get the latest unexpected news, you don't even bat an eye. You say, "I've overcome stuff like this in the past; I will do so again." Nothing will stop me from becoming a bank president or a successful business owner. If however, you shrink from challenge and bemoan the unexpected—?Why me?? Why now??—then you will have nothing in your background to convince you that you can move around all barriers. This will reinforce a negative self-image and lead you to conclude that you are indeed a loser and a victim. It's all in how you treat the unexpected, as a friend or as an enemy, as a teacher or as a bother, as a challenge or as a roadblock. The choice is yours; that much, you can control.

- Don't rush the process of dancing with the unexpected. You don't need to have a solution to a problem right away. You might not see the open window at first glance. That's okay. You might need to ruminate over the unexpected for several days or weeks. Take your time, but guard the attitude that you will figure out how to incorporate the unexpected into your goal attainment, not be waylaid by it. Don't make rash decisions, such as quitting your job or moving out of town, immediately after meeting the unexpected. Digest it for a time, think about how you should process it all, and then make a calm, reasonable decision. You might need to leave your company if it's shrinking and opportunities are disappearing, but don't do that as soon as you hear the quarterly shareholders report. People with the proper self-belief are confident that they will find a way to use the unexpected to their advantage, given enough time.

- As you reflect on the unexpected, don't fail to leave out the possibility that you could have done something to prevent it. You are not in control of all circumstances in the universe, and anyone who tells you otherwise is not telling the truth. But, if you were the first person laid off in this round of cuts, was there a reason? Was it because you were late to work three days out of five? Was it because you refused to be a good team player? This is another way that the unexpected can teach us. It can show us how we DO control our destiny to some degree, and that the unexpected perhaps should have been expected, due to moves we did not make and a standard of conduct we did not live up to.

- Finally, a key part of welcoming the unexpected is understanding that it is not a personal attack on you. This is the false conclusion that many people draw, and it hinders them from fulfilling their potential. As soon as the unexpected enters into their lives, they reason that the world is against them or they just didn't have their cards fall right. These are negative attitudes that will drive you into a black hole fast as you seek to hit your small targets and become the success that you aspire to be.

The unexpected should be your friend, not an enemy, a teacher, not a killer. And, if the unexpected is a piece of great news—you're getting a raise, you're having a baby, your fiancé proposed—then you can realign your small targets and larger objectives for even faster fulfillment.

Chapter 2: Embrace Willpower

You are not going to let the unexpected knock you off track. The ability to recover from unknowns is willpower.

What is willpower? It can mean a lot of things to a lot of people. Let's think of it as mental strength that is built up through discipline. Let's call willpower the force that is generated through proper Mind Hacking.

Here are some of the actions that you can take to embrace willpower to its fullest degree:

- To make sacrifices to build willpower. That means, for instance, turning off a video game to read your chapter on mental growth. That means eschewing those three doughnuts at work to maintain your diet (more on that in the next chapter). That means not dating around anymore when you have a pretty good idea of who you want to marry. Sacrifice hurts for a brief time, but it builds up willpower, which will make you stronger and better prepared to reach your goals.

- In a similar way, you will need to concentrate on self-discipline often to build your willpower reserve. You will need to stay that extra hour at the office to do that extra task that will impress the boss, rather than join the boys for Happy Hour right away. You will need to attend that seminar on leadership one weekend rather than hit the beach when the weather is great. These are examples of the type of self-discipline that you will need to have as you build your willpower. As you say "No" to the good to say "Yes" to the better, you will see that it becomes easier and easier to say "No" to many temptations that used to trip you up and slow you down. They add up fast.

- Another way to build willpower is to refrain from reacting negatively when there is a negative situation or someone is agitating you (for instance, "road rage") to let someone have it verbally or through an email or text (how often have we all done this?). In the short run, it will feel great to tell someone what you really think about him/her, but in the long run it can really screw up your journey. That 10-minute tirade or spicy email can come back to haunt you, in fact it always does. It goes into your file and all of the sudden you are not considered leadership material. Someone always notices, Was it worth it? No. Part of developing willpower is practicing restraint, especially when the unexpected hits you in the face, or the sheer difficulty of dealing with certain people arises again and again.

- Don't let a fear of failure control you. Rather, take "imperfect" decisive action and understand that if you do fail, you can use it as a stepping stone to success, a valuable lesson. If you like anyone else, you probably have struggled with self-doubt. As part of that struggle, you are afraid of adding any failure to the already sizeable load on your shoulders. You need to not see failure as added weight, but rather as a teacher, much like the unexpected that we discussed in the previous chapter. Once you vanquish your fear of failure, you will have the willpower needed to take decisive action at certain points in your life's journey: you will ask the girl to marry you, you will start that side business, you will request a raise and a promotion, take the extra classes. Willpower cannot coexist with a fear of failure, choose one or the other.

- Take physical, tangible actions to grow your willpower. Even though this book is on Mind Hacking, not all of the action points suggested in it are purely mental in nature. It is not recommended that you strive to develop discipline by purposely putting temptation in front of you. For example, if you are on a diet to lose weight, it is not advised to visit bakeries to take in the sights, sounds and smells! However, your discipline should have tangible actions attached to it. If you want to grow your willpower as you seek life change, keep a record of actions you took that demonstrated your commitment to increasing your willpower. Examples would be: booked a place at the positive thinking seminar for a weekend next month; sent my significant other flowers in a determined effort to win her heart; began an IRA at the bank to practice consistent saving and improve my long-term financial outlook. These all take willpower, which grows through action in many cases, not by simply wishing it to increase.

You will find that willpower will be most essential early in your journey towards life change. That's because it might be like an underused muscle. It might not have any tone to it at all as you begin. You will need to lift your discipline and commitment consistently to grow your willpower muscle. With time, you will develop an iron-strong will that cannot be defeated by anything or anyone, but it takes time to build that iron.

Early in your quest to achieve small targets, double down on the discipline to facilitate success. It's sort of like the first days of a diet; early in that new eating regimen, you long for carbs or bread or sweets, whatever you are abstaining from. After a few days and weeks, your cravings subside.

It's the same way with willpower. As it grows, you become inherently more disciplined—a better you. As that self-discipline gains momentum, it becomes unstoppable.

Of course, you will fall short at times. You will give in to the doughnuts, your anger, your pettiness, your selfishness. That just proves that you're human. What is important is that you realize your error and understand that multiple shortcomings in a row can really throw you off track, and that you need to get back on course as soon as possible.

Willpower is not about total absence of weakness, but it is about consistently making good choices and resisting mind-sets and snares that can drag you down. After those three doughnuts, you might awaken your taste for sweets, so you will need to physically stay as far away from doughnuts for the next several weeks. You do that not just to prove that you're strong, but because you have short- and long-term goals to fulfill.

You won't lose those five pounds this month if you keep on gorging on doughnuts, and you have not seen many other bank presidents who are 75 pounds overweight. Both short and long term, you need to abstain from 10 a.m. snacks in the break room. Just because it's there does not mean that you have to eat it! It's not worth missing out on your goals.

If you are not overweight and you're reading this book, let's think about another typical way that you can fall short as you grow in willpower. How about: you will refrain from eating out, and commit to cooking your own food which can save you money long term? There's a true test for the time-constrained person.

Rather, you will put that $100+ in your savings account and prepare for your launch of a small business in a few months. Willpower often must have a logical reason to continue(your why), and it does not function well in people who live by their emotions. You must believe 100% that not eating out everyday will help you to achieve both your short- (saving $200/month) and long-term (launching a small business) goals. So have a big "Why" is part of the equation.

In many ways, willpower sacrifices short-term gratification for long-term happiness. That is the opposite of what many societies tell us, but it is absolutely true. A 50-year marriage is usually much more enjoyable than a 5- year marriage ended by an affair, which usually goes nowhere anyway.

Build your willpower by resisting constant eating out and putting the money in the bank; or by eating chicken salads rather than doughnuts to increase health and lose weight.

By the way, when you do fail and suffer a consequence for it, don't fall back into the mind-set that the stars are not aligned for you. That is a destructive attitude that cannot get you to where you want to go. Your boyfriend or girlfriend has not called in four days because you cursed the person out in anger the last time you were on the phone. You abandoned willpower and said whatever you felt like saying. Now, you are not building your relationship the way you want to, and your goal of marrying that and raising a family is in danger. It has nothing to do with the fate! It has everything to do with you, your actions and the direct consequences of those actions.

When the going gets tough in embracing willpower, try this technique:

Spend some time visualizing what your dream life will look like 5 years from now. Where will you be? What will you be doing? What relationships will you have?

Perhaps you will be in a large suburban home with a family, working from home as you are able at your lucrative business. You will have a tremendous balance between family and work, and you will have plenty of income to enjoy life. 5 years goes by pretty fast.

The only way that you are going to develop that business is by saving money or finding money partners to launch it correctly. When you are buying something that you really don't need that will cost you half of this month's intended savings, picture that big house in the suburbs, or the dream car you want. Buying some unnecessary item will not get you closer to that goal, it will only impede your progress to that life that you have envisioned. So always think about whether or not the action you are doing is going to get you closer to your goals?

Visualization of what you want in life can be a powerful tool in developing willpower. If you spend some time visualizing exactly where you want to be in the future every day for 5-10 minutes, it can help guide you in many daily choices. In fact, there are thousands of books describing how powerful this is and the quick results it can bring if you commit to visualization properly every single day. This practice of visualization will be much more thoroughly covered in Chapter Five.

Embrace willpower and grow it. This aspect of Mind Hacking can take you a long way.

Chapter 3: Prioritization Hacks and Tips

Knowing how to prioritize your tasks is an essential skill in both the workplace and at home, yet so few know how to proceed with it. As a result, very little gets done, and frustration or worse can occur. You'll be happy to know there are hacks for that.

Be sure to read through all of these to see which ones will apply best for you. Some are essentials and others will just help to keep you on track. Combined with the skills from the last chapter, these can empower you to crush your goals and get results.

1. **Create a list of your tasks** - If you are going to prioritize your tasks, you are going to need to make a list first. Start by simply creating a numbered list that we can modify at a later time. Try to make it as concise as possible and leave some space in the ones where further steps may be required.

2. **Know what to remove** - If you are attempting to achieve a particular goal, take a look at your list and determine which items are not immediately required. It is easy to deviate from the original intentions when creating and outlining goals or the tasks associated with them. If you see an item on your list that

doesn't align, cut it. You can always focus on the outliers when you have found the time to complete the original goal.

3. **If overtasked, ask your Boss 'what can wait?'** - Many people are frightened to tell their boss that the workload is simply impossible. If you prepare yourself then this shouldn't be a worry. Go to your manager and advise them that you have two, large and priority tasks that are time-consuming and cannot be accomplished in a quality fashion in the time provided. Then ask, 'Out of these two clients/tasks, which one will have to wait?.' Another way to ask is to say 'This task has a projected timeframe of x days and this other task of x days. I can't do them both at once so who which task do you want me to finish first?.' Despite popular belief, your Manager will typically be quite appreciative if you inform them that timeline estimates may be incorrect and could cause delay in important tasks. This gives them the option to delegate one of the tasks and helps to save them from trouble from their own boss. This is a tactic employed by true professionals when they know without a doubt that a priority task could fall behind schedule so don't be afraid to ask your boss 'Which task will have to wait?'

4. **Learn the difference between immediate and important** - A task can be important and yet not be required immediately. You will want to teach yourself to recognize the difference between something that is merely important and

something that needs to be done RIGHT AWAY. It can seem rather overwhelming if all of the tasks are of high importance but learning this distinction will help you to sort through this quickly. Try making a list with 'Important' tasks on one side and 'Immediate' tasks on the other to get yourself into the habit of identifying them quickly.

6. **Identify from the 'immediate' list which is most important** - Now that you have an 'immediate' list, you must sort these by importance and deadline. This will help you to further prioritize for the next list.

7. **Create your list, divide it into daily, weekly, and monthly tasks** - Create a master list starting with your prioritized 'immediate' list. First create a timeline for the immediate and important items and then you can schedule the rest of your tasks accordingly. Planning ahead in this fashion can allow you to utilize such tools as Outlook and other schedulers to set up reminders for yourself should you be so inclined.

8. **Factor in time involved when deciding which 'immediate' tasks to do** - Don't forget to factor in the time involved in your immediate tasks. This will help you to get a realistic view of what you can actually accomplish in a given time period. You may find that a number of tasks will not fit in the time that you have available, but do not be discouraged.

This is the main function of prioritization, making sure that the most important tasks get done in a timely and efficient manner.

9. **Review your workload on a regular basis** - Your workload can change and goals sometimes must be modified when setbacks or changes in direction occur. Be sure to review your workload daily and be prepared if you need to make some modifications to your planning. This is especially crucial when dealing with items from our 'immediate' list. Since you have those items pre-ranked and time lined, you will be prepared to rearrange as needed with little or no stress. Remember, planning is your friend.

10. **Prepare for 'fires'** - Prepare yourself for contingencies. Perhaps you might get sick or need to take some time away from your task at hand. Plan in advance free-time that can be diverted from leisure to catch up on the tasks at hand. This gives you some leeway should the unexpected occur and can help ease your mind should a setback arise. While you can't predict the future, you can predict some possibilities; it is well worth your while to prepare for all of the problems that you can. Working hard now means less stress later.

11. **Make a deadline calendar** - Creating a calendar where deadlines are visibly marked is a good way to help keep yourself in a production mindset and to help ensure that priority tasks get done. While there are a number of apps that can send us reminders or set off alarms in our pockets, the old-

fashioned calendar with its in-your-face presence is still an extremely useful mind hack to help keep you on track. Best of all, they are inexpensive. So, get yourself a calendar and mark off your deadlines on priority tasks. Color code them and bam, you've got a visual reminder to help to keep you from getting behind. It's a simple mind hack that has stood the test of time.

12. **Let importance win sometimes over urgency** - Occasionally during a project you will find that you have a chance to quickly accomplish a task that is important, though not one of the urgent ones. If it can be done without affecting the deadline for the urgent task, then go ahead and feel free to get it done. With prioritization we are concerned with making sure the urgent come first normally, but there are exceptions. For instance, one of your friends visits from out of town and happens to be an accountant. She offers to help you with some budgetary portion of a project and this will likely save you days of work, but you are currently working on an urgent restructuring of a bid. If you can still meet your deadline, then by all means you should take advantage of the chance to accomplish the important task in less time. As long as you are keeping a productive mentality and meeting your deadlines, it is okay to deviate a little from the plan, but only when extremely advantageous!

13. **Use milestones to see the bigger picture** - Often tasks that we perform for ourselves or for clients are divided not only

into their sub-tasks but also into 'milestones,' named after the markers that Romans used to measure their roads. A milestone is essentially a project phase and is a useful tool for determining overall progress without having to micromanage. When you prioritize your tasks and group them, be sure to designate them into milestones so that your project is both prioritized and phased. This will help you to see or report the bigger picture with ease.

14. **Payment vs. Milestones vs. Urgency** - Sometimes when we are performing a task for a client, we have an urgent task but we also have a single, quick task that is the last required for a milestone (and thus, a payment for your business). Perform the quick task. Nothing boosts morale and productivity quite like getting paid. Yes, the urgent task should have priority in normal cases, but if the urgent task is complicated, you should still perform the milestone task and compensate with a little extra free time put towards the urgent task. Keep motivated, keep profitable and hack your mindset to further success.

15. **Understand breach-of-priority consequences** - Once you have established a hierarchy or your priority items, be sure that it remains unbroken. Various reminders as recommended in this chapter will help to keep it from happening, but that's not enough. To understand the relationship between the prioritized projects and steps, ask yourself 'what happens to my

timeline if this step takes longer than anticipated?.' This gives you a chance to plan for contingencies and helps put you in the necessary mindset to meet your deadlines. Once you've drafted your priorities, plan for the unexpected.

16. **Manage client meddling** - It never fails that once you went through the trouble of prioritizing steps in a particular project, someone is going to force you to address another priority to be done first. You need to resist this whenever possible. If the item prioritized above this request is part of a project, you can consider doing it first, but it is better if you instead explain your prioritization so that they have a better understanding of the overall plan. Remember, they are employing your skill set because you are a professional, so while you can do it their way if they insist, be sure to advise that this may result in more time billed for the project and give a thorough explanation why that is. After this, if they still want to micromanage, hey, why not? They are paying for it. Proper client management will help keep you feeling like the professional that you are and ensure a proper mindset as you proceed to get that work done!

17. **Always request more time than you need** - One little hack to help ensure that your priority deadlines are met is to always request more time than you need. Not a great amount, of course, or you might potentially lose a bid or particular work assignment, but just a small amount to give you a little wiggle

room. This way if something comes up you are prepared and if not, you look great for finishing early. Remember, always request more time than you need. This is one of those hacks that can make you both look good and feel good so consider using this whenever you can.

18. **Prioritize as a Team** - If you will be working with others on a project, consider prioritization as a team. For best results, ask each individual to create their own priority list during the week for a meeting on Friday. Once Friday arrives, each person can go through their list and the team can decide what is the best prioritization for the steps involved. This can be beneficial because all of the team will be on the same page, they will feel that their voices have been heard; and because you will be making the prioritization decisions in an informed manner because you will know all of the skill sets being brought to the table. You might not know offhand that some team members have specialized experience that might come in handy in certain phases of the project and using this method can remedy that and help you streamline the work. Use this hack whenever you can. It's a sure way to a successful project.

19. **Don't be afraid to ask a Mentor** - Don't be afraid to ask a Mentor if you are uncertain in regards to the prioritization of some items. One of the hallmarks of a professional is that if they do not know, they would rather swallow their pride and ask, than do a bad job. Nobody can know everything, so don't be afraid to ask a mentor when you need to. They will respect

you more and you won't need to ask next time, so it's a win-win. They've helped you for all this time, consider the possibility that they have more to offer. The goal is a successful prioritization of your project tasks and ultimately a successful project, so keep your eyes on the prize and do what it takes to WIN!

20. **Prioritization standard for all work** - Create a prioritization standard as your prioritization skills develop. You know what type of tasks will be typically involved in your projects, so creating a template as you go along is just good sense. Just be sure to review it constantly so that you can keep things current and you'll have a useful tool that can help make the process easier every year. Your templates can also be used as training tools for others when you move up in the organization (and creating training materials can also help you do exactly that!), so consider building them as you go along for both your convenience and your success. Templates are an excellent hack for your career and for a good productivity mindset.

Keep in mind that this is a lot of information to process so be sure to take a breath and give yourself a little time to digest and let it sink in. Have yourself a cup of coffee with a notepad and brainstorm a few goal ideas and rough outline portions if you like but nothing too serious yet unless you just can't help yourself.

In our next chapter we have even more useful information. They say that a goal without a plan and productivity is actually just 'a dream,' but have no fear, we've got you covered.

Healthy Lifestyle

Drink lots of water

Drinking water not only hydrates the body, but also boosts mental performance. The brain consists of around 85% water and has many ways to tell you when it is dehydrated, such as headaches, brain fog, fatigue, problem to focus or memorize things, depression, insomnia, anger, etc.

When you are thirsty, the brain will already begin to shut down, causing cognitive constraints. So, drink water regularly throughout the day to keep your mental state in working order. *You'd be surprised how something as simple as staying hydrated can make a huge difference in your energy and mental performance.*

Consume brain-boosting foods

The brain needs fuel just as the body does. A well-balanced diet is important for a healthy brain.

Here are some nutritional tips to boost brainpower:

Omega-3 Fatty Acid: Omega-3 fatty acids are essential for a healthy brain. They improve memory, protect the brain against disorders such as dementia and might even reverse the effects of memory loss. Rich sources include tuna, salmon, sardines, and other seafoods. If you don't like seafood, there are other options such as spinach, soybeans, broccoli, walnuts and a big one: Flax meal or flax seeds. Since the body can't produce these types of fatty acids on its own, you will have to include it in your diet. It is recommended to eat these types of ingredients at least three times a week. A deficiency will cause poor memory, fatigue, poor circulation, mood swings, and other problems that will affect your behavior ad thinking abilities.

Do not to consume high dosages. Just because something is good, doesn't mean you should go overboard. Too much Omega-3 fatty acids might increase the risk of a hemorrhagic stroke, which causes a capillary in the brain to rupture or bleed. So, as everything in life, you should keep a balance.

Eat fruits and vegetables: These foods contain lots of antioxidants that protect the cells in your brain from damage. The more colorful the fruits and vegetables are, the better the nutritional benefits.

Limit saturated fat and calories: Saturated fat refers to products such as butter, cream, cheese, and red meat. If your diet includes high dosages of these products, your memory and concentration might weaken and also increase your risk of dementia.

Drink green tea: A powerful antioxidant in green tea, called polyphenols, protect the brain cells against free radicals. Regular consumption might even enhance mental alertness, slow down aging, and enhance memory.

Sleep

People usually sacrifice sleep in order to get more things done. But that extra bit of work or study isn't worth it. Getting the right amount of sleep is important for mental health.

When you're sleep-deprived it is impossible to gain the right set of focus to learn something efficiently and is known to impact reasoning and decision-making functions.

Sleep itself also play a huge role in strengthening the memory, which is crucial for absorbing new information. When we have learned something, sleeping will work on converting those short-term memories into long-term so that the information still feels fresh when we wake up.

Sleeping in 90 minutes intervals, the length of a sleep cycle, is preferred to wake up more alert.

Consistent exercise

There are plenty of reasons why you should exercise. You might want to lose weight, build muscles, or just

be healthy. But exercise can also help you learn better by boosting thinking and memory in both direct and indirect ways. This has been proven by science.

Directly, exercise benefits the brain by reducing inflammation, insulin resistance, and stimulates growth factors in the brain.

Indirectly, exercise helps by reducing stress and improving sleep, which often disrupts the ability to learn.

Studies also show that people who exercise have an increased volume in the parts of the brain that controls memory and thinking.

To reap the benefits, you should at least get half an hour of moderate exercise a day. Walk, swim, climb the stairs, dance -- anything that gets the heart pumping would do. For the best results, exercise in the morning. This will spike brain activity to absorb new information faster, prepare you for mental stress, and handle situations better.

Identify health problems

Nothing prevents us more from concentrating than when we are feeling sick, especially if we are taking a bunch of medicine that further impairs the mind. If you don't even feel like procrastinating, then you are really in trouble if work needs to be done or have an exam coming up. Here are a few tips on how to make the best of the situation:

- Don't overwhelm yourself or you might feel even worse. Break up your work into smaller chunks of 15 to 30 minutes at a time.
- Do the easy tasks first or you will just tire yourself out sooner. Make flashcards and organize your notes to tackle the more difficult things.
- Get enough sleep. You will heal faster when you allow your mind and body some rest.
- Always be prepared that something might happen. Plan your schedule ahead of time so that you don't have to do everything all at once.

<u>Laugh</u>

Laughter might be the best medicine to boost your learning, just as the saying goes. Forgot something? Just laugh it off. Humor engages multiple areas of the brain, including the part that is vital for learning and creativity. It also increases mood, lowers blood pressure, and reduces stress. The less stressed we are, the better our memory.

When we laugh, or just enjoy some humor, dopamine is sent to the brain through the increase in endorphins. This provides the brain with a sense of reward and pleasure, which changes brain wave activity to the point of amplifying memory and recall.

Focus & Motivation

<u>Motivation and goals</u>

A lack of motivation will automatically make it more difficult to stay focused on studying or getting any work done. Without something to drive you, there can be no success. Look at how easy those same people who struggle to concentrate learn names, locations, etc. on movies, TV shows, and games without any real effort. That's because they are entertained and actually want the information they so easily absorb. Whereas a lack of motivation will just reject information we are trying to force into the mind.

<u>There are two types of motivation:</u>

Intrinsic motivation: When we are internally motivated by something we enjoy or think that it is important. People with this type of motivation are happy with their work or studies because it is a challenge they look forward to even if there is no promised reward.

Extrinsic motivation: When people work or study because of external circumstances such as for rewards or punishment. This type of motivation is a negative influence and won't help the person improve.

When you are lacking motivation, try to focus on a goal you really desire. What are you trying to accomplish, what is "your" why? Always keep the bigger picture in your mind rather than looking at the work itself.

Don't over think. You will make things more complicated than it really is by anticipating problems that might never happen. It also creates unnecessary stress which ultimately blocks motivation and focus. Break down your objectives into smaller chunks so you can feel as if you are accomplishing more.

Deal with mental blocks. Nothing brings down motivation faster than the feeling that you can't do anything right. Negativity often creates this loop in your mind which prevents you from digging into your creativity at will. Unblock yourself by looking at the situation from a different perspective.

On the same note, you should stop being negative overall. Do you sometimes scan through an assignment and anticipate how difficult it would be to accomplish? Having such a mindset already sets you back and sucks all motivation you might have had. Train your mind to think positive. Just imagine how you are going to enjoy the challenge and it will feel lighter already.

Regularly recall all your accomplishments. This will encourage you to work harder and enhance focus. The more you think about those memories of success, the more you would want to experience such moments again. This really works, in fact, try to experience future memories of success too.

Meditate

Meditation is a popular stress and relaxation technique. But it also increases the mind's ability to focus for long durations. With ongoing multitasking and pressure in today's society, it becomes very difficult to concentrate. Increasing this ability can improve problem-solving skills and creativity. People who don't understand meditation think that it means to sit down and do nothing. But that's not true. It is an active form of mind training.

Here are a few ways how meditation affects the brain:

1. **Depression and stress:** Meditation can have the same effect as antidepressants on the mind. That doesn't make it a magic solution to depression and anxiety, though. It is simply a tool that helps you manage the symptoms. The calmer your mind, the clearer your thoughts will be.

2. **Volume changes:** Meditation can change the brain structure by increasing the cortical thickness in the part of the mind that controls memory and learning. And also decreases the volume in the part that controls stress and fear.

3. Concentration: One of the main benefits of meditation aims to improve focus. A study confirms that in only a few days of regular meditation, there's already a small improvement.

4. Brain age: As we age, the brain automatically deteriorates. But through regular meditation it is possible to slow down the process.

If you don't like to meditate, then simply turn off the lights. Sitting in the dark can create a similar effect and can even make you more aware. Start with basic breathing exercises, you'd be surprised how just doing this will affect you.

Chapter 4: Meditation and Mindfulness Hacks

When we think of meditation, we tend to visualize a happy Buddhist priest, sitting in a lotus position and serenely contemplating the universe. Sounds great but it also sounds like a complicated thing. You'll be glad to know that anyone can meditate and best of all, it doesn't have to be complicated or time-consuming. So, what about this Mindfulness stuff? Mindfulness is similar to meditation, as it is largely based on some Buddhist meditative practices, but with a modern twist. The aim of Mindfulness is getting yourself centered and dealing with 'cognitive distortions,' which is just fancy psych-speak for 'incorrect assumptions/illogical thoughts.' Mindfulness helps you to get yourself back in good order when these cognitive distortions or even general stress occur. That said, we've compiled a list of meditations and mindfulness techniques that you can do at home or in the workplace. Give them a try and see which ones work best for you. A little universal harmony can really work wonders for hacking your mindset!

1. **Mindful Munching** - Pick a time when you are eating alone. It can be a snack break or if you really want a nice

experience, choose breakfast, lunch, or dinner. Clear your mind and simply focus on the aspects of your meal that are so familiar already you might have forgotten how to fully enjoy them. First, focus on the scents, then taste and texture. Don't allow your thoughts to wander. If you find an external thought creeping in then quickly take a drink of your beverage and distract yourself with contemplation of the taste, temperature, and scent of this. Continue slowly until you finish your meal and you will find yourself quite refreshed and ready to focus on the day ahead.

2. **Personal mantra** - Develop a personal mantra for yourself. This can be any old set of words, for example, the Wizard of Oz classic quote 'There's no place like home,' the important part is the meaning that you associate with it. When you are enjoying something, you can repeat this mantra to reinforce the good items that you wish to associate with it. Associate visual cues, like a nice sunset or a starry sky. Associate scents and tastes, like gramma's baked cookies. Then in times of stress at the workplace or home you can simply close your eyes for a moment and repeat your mantra a few times and let the memories rush through you. This one is nice because you can carry it with you anywhere.

3. **3 Minute breath-count** - Set a timer for 3 minutes on your smartphone, personal computer, or kitchen timer. Next, simply close your eyes and count your breaths. Breathe in, one,

breathe out, two, and so on and so on. When the timer goes off, open your eyes and you will find yourself surprisingly relaxed, as if you'd taken a one-hour nap and magically squeezed it into 3 minutes!

4. **Visualize a swiftly growing tree** - Visualization is a powerful meditative tool. Sit somewhere you are comfortable and close your eyes. Imagine an acorn dropping from the sky and landing on the ground. Swiftly taking root and growing into a mighty oak over the course of a few minutes. See the bark as it lightens and the tree widens, its branches reaching up to the sky and moving further apart as it grows taller and taller still. See the tree dropping acorns and visualize the spreading of an oak grove if you like, or when the oak is fully grown then let yourself hear the birds, crickets, and other sounds of nature nearby. When you feel suitably relaxed, simply open your eyes and go about your day.

5. **Follow the lights behind your eyes** - This technique is good for reaching a meditative state and also, incidentally, may be used at night to help you sleep if you have the occasional bout of insomnia. When we close our eyes, there are traces of 'light' that we see behind our eyelids because our eyes are always trying to collect data. What you will want to do is to imagine that you are a hunter, chasing the light that you see behind your eyes, and that you must clear your mind of thoughts because these thoughts will alert the lights to your

presence. The easiest way to avoid thinking is to focus solely on silence and the lights, as if you were running behind them in your mind. It takes a bit of time to master but this technique is a very powerful means of clearing your mind so that you ferret out distractions and negative thoughts. Give it a try!

6. **Smile** - The simple act of smiling is actually meditative in itself. Call centers often train their employees to smile when they are speaking on the phone, as the 'smile can be heard' in the call. There is data to back up that this is effective. For some reason, even a forced smile can elevate the mood. If you aren't the type that likes to smile, just spin your viewpoint with this thought. Sometimes you are smiling and sometimes you are showing the world your teeth.

7. **Just the facts** - An easy exercise you can do in any environment to get yourself centered is to take a mental inventory of your surroundings. Look around and note the color of the walls, the kind and texture of the floor. How tall or short are the people around you. What are their facial features, hair colors, and choices of clothing?

8. **Emotion rainbow** - When sorting through a number of distracting emotions, this is an excellent exercise to get yourself mobile again. Visualize each emotion that you are feeling as a color in a personal rainbow. You can use traditional assignments, such as red for anger, blue for sadness, or simply assign whatever comes to mind. Visualize them top to bottom

from strongest to weakest and once you are holding this image in your head, try to make the negative colors seem smaller by enlarging the positive ones. This can help you to elevate your moods by the simple acknowledgment of what you are feeling and the positive affirmation of what you choose to feel.

9. **3-3-3 breathing** - Breathe in for a count of 3, hold it in for a count of 3, and breathe out for a count of 3. Once you master this, try mixing it up. Breathe in for a count of 4, hold it for 4, exhale for 5... Play with these techniques and you will find that certain breathing patterns will calm you or invigorate you through moderation of the brain's oxygen levels. Some people report that this can become automatic over time and kick-in automatically in times of stress so don't hesitate to try this out for yourself. You'll be very pleased with the results.

10. **Muscle tensing from top to bottom-** This is a popular and fairly easy meditative technique that you can try. Start by flexing the muscles in your feet and then relaxing them. Move up to your calves and then your thighs, slowly up your body until you have gone as high as you can. This provides a distraction focus that can get your mind off of the every day and help you to focus inward. As such, it is a useful trick to have at your disposal.

11. **Shower meditation** - This is a simple meditation that you can do anytime that you are taking a shower. Close your eyes and as you clean imagine that the stresses of your day are

falling from you and going down the drain. As each one disappears, think of yourself becoming more and more like a fresh slate, ready to face the day new and relaxed.

12. **Self-Contemplative Mindfulness** - This mindfulness technique is a way to better get to know yourself. Set a timer for 5 minutes, lay down, close your eyes, and relax. Spend time asking yourself 'who am I?' but don't put too much thought into it. Focus on repeating the question like a mantra and feel what impressions it produces in you. When the timer finishes (which can happen pretty quickly if you are in the right mental state), write down the impressions that you received. Even just a list of words is fine. This is a good way for gauging your inner state and learning more about yourself.

13. **Prism walk** - Take a walk in the park and focus, at first on nothing, but your breathing and the nature around you. As thoughts intrude, see yourself as a prism, and allow these thoughts to diffuse as light diffuses through the prism. In this way, you are symbolically breaking down your stresses via visualization and with a little practice, this can be a great way to de-stress.

14. **Five-Sense Grounding** - This exercise is a mindful way to ground yourself when you are feeling stressed, panicked, or angry. Think of something for each of your senses that you can readily bring to mind. Something that you have seen, like a favorite sunrise or an exotic location. Something that you have

touched, like the feel of velvet or grains of sand. Something that you have tasted, like bitter lime or fresh cherries. Something you've heard, like a recent song or perhaps your child singing. Lastly, think of a scent, perhaps the fresh baking smells from visiting a grandparent or the smell of a new leather jacket. This is a good exercise too for when you are feeling overwhelmed. If there is no time to go through all the senses, a quick mental 1 or 2 should still help to get you centered so that you don't find yourself making an emotional decision or mistakes at work.

15. **Pet your pet** - A meditation for those who simply can't or don't like standard meditation, the act of petting your pet has a similar meditative effect. Stroking the fur of your cat or dog produces feel-good chemicals in your brain, such as oxytocin, prolactin, and serotonin. It also leads to happier animals at home, so consider this if you don't like to go the meditative or mindfulness route.

16. **Temporary beginner mindset** - As a Mindfulness thinking exercise for problem-solving, ask yourself how you would approach this problem if you were a novice. They say that you can teach a novice, but never an expert, so what we are hoping to accomplish is a little mindful thinking outside of the box. Roleplaying is a good way to accomplish this. Imagine how a friend who is not an expert in your field would go about solving your problem. While the answer may be largely wrong,

forcing yourself to think in this fashion can help you to figure out alternate ways to solve your dilemma. Sometimes the best mental hacks involve a disconnect so try this one for yourself and see what kind of results you receive.

17. **Nature's Daily Mascot** - Make a note each day of the first animal that you see on your commute to work (your pets don't count, unless you have more than one and really want them to). As the day proceeds, when stress comes your way, visualize this animal. Recall what details that you can about it. How large was it? If it was a bird, was it singing? Use this as a way to pull you out of your routine. Recalling something as random as the first animal of the day can help get you focused and best of all, it is fairly random, so this technique tends to keep its efficacy.

18. **Practice outcome-based thinking** - An excellent Mindfulness technique that you can practice is outcome-based thinking. Visualize the outcome that you desire and spend some time adding as much detail as possible. The theory behind this is that the better you can envision the outcome, the easier it will be to map your steps to it. Give it a try and think big, see what you can build with this mind hack!

19. **Meditative housework** - When you are doing your housework, clear your thoughts and simply focus on the work itself. The texture of the washcloth when cleaning the dishes. The smell of dust when vacuuming and how it warms the carpet. The sounds of nature when you are taking out the trash.

Don't let external thoughts intrude but rather, take mindful notice of what is around you. This can be quite relaxing and makes the housework go surprisingly fast as well. Try it for yourself and see!

20. **Musical brainstorm** - When attempting some problem solving, try getting a little help from your subconscious. Get a notepad and a pen and select a few minutes' worth of songs to listen to, preferably instrumental. Close your eyes and think of the problem that you are trying to solve. As you listen to the music, let it carry you, but keep the problem in the back of your mind. As solutions occur to you, write a single word in the notepad as a reminder of it, close your eyes, and let it go. When the musical score is complete, see how many solutions you have compiled and feel free to flush them out. This is a particularly useful exercise as the music opens the left side of your brain, associated with creativity. Give it a go when you are trying to solve a particularly difficult problem, you might find yourself very pleased with the results.

There we go. We hope that you will try some of these techniques to hack your mindset a little to keep some order and harmony close to you at all times. We were discussing mediation (but that was Zen and this is now), so we shall proceed to our next chapter where we will discuss the benefits of organization. Don't worry, we don't expect you to clean the house from top to toe, but rather we have a number of hacks to give your house or workspace a more minimalist and practical feeling to it that will help hack your mindset to even further productivity levels while also enhancing the comfort levels of the humble home.

Chapter 5: Baby-Steps to Disciplining Yourself - Mental Changes

In this chapter, we shall put to practice all that we know about self-discipline. Since most actions are cultivated in the mind first, it is only fair that we begin with the mental changes that we need to make in order to become more self-disciplined in life.

However, this isn't going to be easy and neither something that you can learn in a day. It is going to take time and involve little changes to be made. The key is persistence, something we shall learn more about in detail later in this chapter. Like any other skills, this too needs training. The stronger you practice, the stronger you will get. Think of it as an exercise. You start with the basics and then move onto the harder stuff. Also, stop when you think you can't perform, which means you can't overdo it out either. You need breaks in between too.

First things first, every great idea is born in the mind. From there, with a solid execution plan, it is built and worked upon on paper and later comes the practical implementation of it. Thus, we are going to start with the execution first as well.

Build an Execution Plan

In order to start practicing self-discipline, you must have a clear vision of the goals and objectives you hope to accomplish with it. Perhaps, you want to learn self-discipline to quit smoking, stay away from unhealthy eating, resist the urge to shop, or control your anger. You need to know why you want to disciple yourself. Moreover, you need to visualize what success would look like once you have learned to be disciplined. Having a visual will keep you motivated towards the task at hand. The reason for having a clear execution plan is essential is because sometimes it is easier to get lost when we don't know where we are going.

A clear execution plan also outlines all the steps you need to set and tick off from your list to reach your ultimate goal. Wondering why this step is so crucial in the process of building self-discipline? Here are some convincing reasons to get you on track.

A sound execution plan helps you:

Achieve Faster and Measurable Results

Having a clear plan gives you a purpose to look forward to. A life without purpose is wasteful. If you don't have anything to look forward to and hope that you may achieve 'something' someday is like having only an impetus but not knowing where to use it.

A clear plan allows you to shift your focus from the 'what' aspect of things to the 'how' aspect. It means making small changes every day. For instance, if it is your anger that you need to discipline, you can begin with outlining everyday goals like, "I won't shout at anybody today" or "I will talk politely with everyone at the office today." This seems small at first, but once you turn this into a habit, you will notice a positive change in your temperament over time.

Once you begin noticing these changes, it will add to your motivation and you will find yourself seeking more from life.

Improve Your Attitude

Having an execution plan puts you in the driver's seat. You take full control of your life and how you want it to be. Since you have chosen a goal of your own preference, you are more likely to feel positive about its completion and success. When we begin to see our goals in an active state, we feel even more motivated to keep going. An experiment on animals around goal setting revealed that when we are closer to achieving our goals, the neurotransmitter dopamine guides the system towards the completion. These signals become stronger as the achievement of the goal is closer (Howe, Tierney, Sandberg, Phillips, & Graybiel, 2013).

Stay Focused

An execution plan in action gives you a point of focus. This focal point allows you to make the best use of your available resources so that you can maximize the output with calculated input. After all, you don't want to end up wasting your resources and energy on whimsical things that prevent you from becoming self-disciplined in life.

Avoid Procrastinating

If we were to list the top-most damaging quality to advancement, it would be procrastination. A focused plan prevents that from happening. Procrastination makes a person distracted and lazy. He/she keeps putting things off to another hour, day, or week which results in lost focus. <u>The loss of focus leads to failure</u>. Therefore, the best way to avoid this chain of events from preventing you to become self-disciplined<u>, is to have a plan of action at all times with small objectives to accomplish.</u> That way, you will remain focused and motivated and not delay doing things that need to be done.

Manage Your Time Better

Taking things forward from the aforementioned point, an execution plan in place prevents waste of time. Having a plan ensures that each of the tasks gets an allotted time-frame which enables you to stay true to your goals. When you keep completing each task within the allotted time-frame, more work will get done. If there aren't any key tasks, an execution plan will help you juggle between the many things that need to be done, helping you prioritize. This way, you will also be able to track any redundant or unproductive activities that you may avoid altogether to save you time and ultimately help you become self-disciplined.

Make Sound Decisions

You will be able to decide better when faced with multiple choices with an execution plan. For instance, deciding whether you should go watch television or work on your goals will become easier. You will know exactly how much time you need to invest to achieve your goals and thus every choice you make will beg the question, "does it get me closer to my goals?" first.

Stay Motivated

It is important to understand that in order to achieve anything in life, we all need a "push." Something that drives us, keeps us moving forward, makes us test our limits, etc. Motivation is the driving force that makes all this happen. To accomplish anything in your life, you need the motivation to stick to it and take it till the end. But motivation needs to come from the heart. It needs to be constant. It doesn't have to be something that inspires you for a day only. When it is straight from the heart and towards something you really need, only then you will be able to sustain your vision and move towards your end goal.

Measure Your Progress

Like any new website, it needs metrics to track its visitors, their preferred landing pages, time spent on the website, etc., even your goals need to be measured with time to see how far you have come from where you first began. Measuring the progress not only serves as a motivational factor, but it also allows you to gain insights about how much effort you have put in already and how much effort you need to put in further before you discipline yourself.

Establish Accountability

Having an execution plan makes you active. Rather than just talking about how you need to learn self-discipline, you actually commit to it by being accountable. Becoming accountable means that you will become your own boss and assess your weaknesses and shortcomings. **Did you know according to research, individuals who simply thought about a goal succeeded 50% less time in achieving them than those who had them written (Hale, 2011).**

That is how important it is to have an execution plan from the start. Since your goal is to become self-disciplined, starting with an execution plan will surely get you there.

Set boundaries

Setting boundaries is also an essential part of learning self-discipline. If you don't know when to say no to someone or things that waste time and energy, you will have a difficult time achieving your goal. A lot of people struggle with the same and give up earlier than they should only because they overburden themselves with unnecessary chaos.

With an execution plan in motion, it helps you draw a line where needed so that you don't give in to distractions and also let go of people who push you down and impede your progress. Boundaries and limitations also help you analyze the things that are stopping you from achieving your goals.

Overcome Stress

One of the biggest challenges to self-discipline is disorganization. Not understanding how things are going to work, how are you going to achieve your goals, or what plan of action will work best to get you through are all those questions that you must answer before you begin. Now, imagine you don't have a clear execution plan? What will happen? How will you determine which steps to take or what to do?

You will begin stressing over it and might even lose focus. Even the simplest of tasks will seem difficult and add to your stress.

Enhance Communication

Having a clear execution plan also helps others understand what you are trying to achieve. If you are closely associated with other people in your life, whatever decisions you take will have an effect on them as well. Knowing what to expect, they can be on board with you as well. Moreover, they might even join in and motivate you to reach your goal, i.e. to become self-disciplined.

Practice Persistence

Ever had that feeling like you should just quit? Maybe, it was a very tough workout session where you felt you were about to die? Or perhaps, it was too much to see other people enjoying hearty steaks while you swallowed your dry leafy salad?

There are times in our lives when we stand on the edge of giving up. Yet, we don't. What keeps us going is our persistence. Persistence is the ability to keep on thriving even when you don't feel like it.

It especially happens when we are trying to challenge our habits and do something we usually don't. For instance, if you are someone who loves to eat out, you might find it difficult to remain indoors and cook. If you are a shopaholic, it may seem impossible to not go into the next shop and not buy another pair of shoes you don't need or hurt your feet too much.

When we resist such temptations and continue to do so for a long time, our motivation waxes and wanes like tides hitting the shore. There are days when you feel most confident about achieving your goals and then there are days you just want to curl up in your bed and stay there.

Nonetheless, it isn't always motivation that keeps you on your toes, it is your actions that keep you going for it. Persistence keeps you moving. It keeps pushing you to take action even when you are running low on motivation.

It is believed that persistence offers its own motivation. The idea behind this is that since you will continue taking actionable steps, you will get results. Positive results are in itself a source of motivation. Imagine you are trying to lose weight. You come across all the motivational articles that pump your adrenaline and keep telling you it's possible for you too. However, if you won't see any results, will you still remain motivated despite all the knowledge you have? Probably not. You will want to see results, which is only possible when you remain persistent. Even shedding the first few pounds will serve as an extra boost of motivation, especially when you feel that you are able to fit in those old skinny jeans of yours. Would you still need to read any articles or hear any inspirational speeches from athletes?

Another important thing to note here is that while we try to remain persistent and take action, not all outcomes are in our favor. Sometimes, even the best of efforts result in failure. Setbacks are just roadblocks that you must cross when on the road to success. Even in the darkest of times, we must remain optimistic and look at the brighter side of things. Every failure is a lesson and lessons prevent mistakes from happening in the future.

So when faced with a setback, rather than blaming others for it or making excuses, we must take responsibility for it. Messed up a project at work? No need to go in with your resignation letter in your hand. Accept that you made a mistake and are willing to correct it. Ate a whole tub of ice-cream when you weren't supposed to? No need to feel guilty. Instead, own your mistake and try to avoid it the next time. Try to recall the guilt you felt so that you don't end up doing it again.

Staying Persistent Amidst the Setbacks

Do you know the difference between a successful person and a failure? The one who fails feels sorry for themselves. The one who succeeds learns from their actions and uses that as a lesson for the future. Every failure, obstacle, or problem comes with a seed of opportunity or benefit.

If you are trying to build self-discipline, you must first become persistent. Here are some ways to get you started.

Take Inspiration from Others

Isn't it so refreshing to read about the life of someone who started with nothing and ended up with everything?

Like motivation, inspiration is another driving force to keep you persistent. Learning about someone's journey, about the hardships they faced, and tactics they used to overcome them allows you to get inspired and strive for the same. It wasn't easy for them. However, they remained persistent and didn't give up. If you wish to be as successful as them, you need to become as persistent as them.

Find People on the Same Boat as You

Having a partner to motivate you, push you, and encourage you to keep moving is a blessing in disguise. Moreover, if you happen to find someone who shares the same obstacles in life as you, the two of you can become each other's prime support. Add to that the valuable lessons you two can learn from each other so that you don't have to come face to face with them later in life.

Don't Stress Over It

Stress is like a mental leak. You can't let it come in the way of your persistence. Reducing stress should be your prime concern. Failing to reduce it will eventually lead to a demotivated state. Another important reason why you need to manage your stress levels is that stress makes you lose energy. The more stress you feel, the larger the amount of cortisol in your body. The presence of cortisol in high quantity triggers antibodies that then need to restore balance in the body. All this results in the loss of energy which makes one feel fatigued. A fatigued person can't stay persistent for long.

Handle failure with Confidence

It is a given that you must come across some roadblocks that cause a setback. Setbacks can result in loss of motivation and ultimately cause you to give up altogether. We can't let that happen. Therefore, it is important that we understand how to handle a setback. This will make you remain persistent and make the best use of available resources.

It Will Not Be Any Easier

A lot of times, the reason people fail to reach their desired goals is that they expected too much from themselves. The wrong expectations can really end up demotivating you. You must understand that not everything will always go as planned and you might need to change the course of everything. You might even have to redo things differently which means starting all over again. So, when you realize that reality isn't how you expected or imagined it to be, that is the time when you need to stick with persistence. You cannot lose heart at this point no matter what.

Moreover, don't have such high expectations that even you, fail to accomplish them.

It's Not a Day's Work

You must never underestimate the length of the problem you face. For instance, if you are trying to discipline yourself from eating too much or having a bad temper, you need to know that overcoming this isn't a day's work. When you are trying to learn how to be self-disciplined there is no such thing as quick or instant success. Each step will take time and energy.

Know Why You Are Doing This

As discussed in the earlier chapter, having a compelling "why" is what is going to get you going. It is also the same with persistence. With every obstacle challenging you, you need something to keep pushing you forward. That will be your "why." Unless you have a purpose to achieve, you won't know what you are doing and why you are doing it. The bigger your reason, the better you will perform.

Acknowledge Your Shortcomings

We aren't perfect, even when we think we are. Being flawed isn't a sign of weakness. It doesn't mean you are a failure. Being aware of what you lack or what you need to work upon is where your strength lies. Shortcomings may not always be your fault. Sometimes, things don't go as planned. Then what do you do? Do you just give up? No!

You learn from those mistakes and circumstances and work towards not letting it happen again. Every weakness or shortcoming is a sign that you are moving forward and acknowledging the changes you need to make in order to reach your goal.

What Will Happen When You Acknowledge Your Shortcomings

However, how do you go about acknowledging and working on your shortcomings? More importantly, what amazing things will happen when you do so?

Let's find out!

A Gateway of Opportunities Will Open

In order to work upon your weaknesses, you need to fully embrace them. Doing so will help you embark upon new opportunities whilst making positive changes in your life. It doesn't matter what you do with them once you have found them. You can either conceal them or let things go as they are going or work on them. Whichever way you choose later, acknowledging them is the first step.

It must be noted that working on your shortcomings can guarantee amazing results. Have you ever wondered that perhaps it is your low self-esteem that hinders your chances of top prosperity and success of your goals? If so, imagine what will happen when you turn it into your strength?

But what if the weakness or shortcomings can't be worked upon? What if it can't be changed? What will you do then?

As stated above, just the acknowledgement alone can do wonders for you. Sometimes having the courage to accept it is what is required to let you know you need to alter your path. For instance, say your weakness lies in being too anxious? You will most likely not be good at tasks that require patience and time. So rather than opting for means that are difficult for you to handle, you may end up finding another way to accomplish them. At the end of the day, you will still be able to reach your goals and be persistent about it. Isn't that the overall goal here?

Your Ego Will Diminish

Pride, an expression that hinders many important decisions of our lives. It stops us from acknowledging our shortcomings and fears. We are afraid of opening up in front of others as we believe that in doing so, we will allow them to see us as weak. This results in defensive acts whenever someone reminds us of that we lack or fear.

Sometimes, we don't even realize that we are being defensive over things that we can actually change about ourselves. For instance, if someone tells us that we are always pessimistic about things in life, we take it to heart immediately and try to avoid talking to that person altogether the next time. How about instead, we critically evaluate ourselves and prove them wrong by being optimistic? It may hurt your ego at first, but it will help you later in life when you come across fears and circumstance you didn't prepare for. Then, this optimism will help you see the light at the end of the tunnel rather than covering your eyes and embracing the darkness.

You'll Discover Your Fears

Fears are often disguised as weaknesses. This means that when you are trying to acknowledge your weaknesses, you are, in a way, dealing with your fears too. When trying to achieve anything in life, we must always ask ourselves this question, "Am I just scared to try this or am I actually bad at it?"

Most of the time, it will be the fear that stops you. However, we don't know it yet or aren't ready to accept it. We usually avoid things because we think we are just bad at them or have failed to accomplish them earlier.

This clarification is critical if you wish to acknowledge your shortcomings and once you do, it will become much easier to stay focused and persistent.

You'll Build Meaningful Relationships

Embracing weaknesses also helps with better communication with others. One of the most common reasons why relationships don't last is that both partners aren't willing to show each other their vulnerability. It should be noted that every counselling session persuades couples to be open with themselves and discuss the root causes of things. That also includes talking about what makes them vulnerable or afraid. Once you let that out, you will notice that your partner will not only admire your courage but it will also show sincerity towards the relationship.

Another benefit of embracing your shortcomings is that people will become more comfortable around you and try to avoid things that make you uncomfortable or hesitant. In short, they will try to support you and encourage you to be more open and discuss what bothers you and what doesn't, making communication more meaningful and your relationship stronger than before.

You'll Acquire Compassion

Ever felt inadequate about your weakness? Ever felt ashamed because of it or tried to hide it?

Occasionally, people try to avoid people and circumstances that allow others to see them as weak. You may avoid attending parties because you are shy. You think that if you do go and try to initiate a conversation, you might end up embarrassing yourself.

It is okay if you feel that way. There are a million others who feel the same way. But should that stop you from going altogether? How will you work on it if you won't acknowledge it as a weakness?

Addressing it will allow you to go easy on yourself and build self-compassion. If you don't like yourself or think that you are too weak to accomplish anything in your life, you may end up proving yourself right.

You Won't Shy Away In Seeking Help

A lot of times, we feel defensive when reminded of our weaknesses. We instantly feel like we are being judged or mocked. But once we embrace our weaknesses and view them as something that should be worked upon, we start a process of seeking help. Things that previously offended us changes to ideas and advice. You begin seeking help and taking opinions of others into consideration without needing to react. When you own your weaknesses, you allow some room for growth.

Remove Stumbling Blocks

Take the biography of any successful leader or philanthropist, you will learn a great deal about self-discipline from them. What problems they faced, how they overcame them with persistence and confidence, what hurdles they crossed, what barriers they broke, etc. All of this is a testament of how crucial it is to learn self-discipline and practice it in all phases of our lives.

If you dream of becoming as successful as them, you need to work on yourself. Now that we already have an execution plan, learned the role persistence plays, and acknowledged our weaknesses, the next step involves getting rid of any distractions that interrupt your focus. Distractions can lead you astray, prohibit you to face your fears and make facing challenges impossible.

Therefore, when trying to learn self-discipline, it is pivotal that we stay away from any distracting elements and try our best to remove them from our lives.

<u>5 Super Distracting Blocks to Avoid</u>

What things are considered distractions? Let's take a look below.

1. Giving into Temptations

We know by now that temptations are nothing but means of distractions. Be it eating a tub of Ben & Jerry's, watching a freshly-released episode of your favorite TV series, missing out on your workout routine in the morning so that you can sleep in a little longer, or wasting time scooping around from one article to another instead of finishing your assignment are all forms of distractions that are rooted from temptations.

All of these examples take your focus away from the actual goal – building self-discipline. Self-discipline requires that you perform one thing over and over again without complaints, boredom, or guilt until it becomes a habit.

Beating temptations is hard but with fulfilling rewards, it becomes a possibility. However, failing to resist them only paves way to demotivation and failure. Even if you don't feel like it, the key is to stick to whatever goal you wish to achieve so that one day, when you look back, you don't have any regrets.

2. Losing Heart Too Soon

Giving up too soon is one of the primary reasons that hinder one's path to achieving self-discipline. Things won't happen for you overnight. You won't lose weight, you won't control your temper, you won't stop lying, and you won't quit smoking. All of these require time and persistence. It is natural to feel frustrated when you don't see things happen the way you thought they would. There are a hundred reasons why things go wrong but only one that leads to complete failure – giving up too quickly.

Even if your self-esteem hits a new low, you mustn't stop fighting and continue to move forward. Try setting smaller and practical goals with a realistic timeline. Next, just stick to it no matter what.

3. Stress

Many psychologists believe that stress is indirectly proportional to self-discipline. How many times have you made the right choice when stressed out or anxious? Not many. Whenever we are stressed, it feels like our brain has stopped working. And to be clear, it isn't always mental stress that gets in the way of things. Sometimes, even physical stress causes problems. Acute or chronic stress are two types of physical stress in which the normal functioning of the body is modified. The symptoms may include headaches, dizziness, panic attacks, etc. It can be episodic or permanent. Episodic stress may be caused by things as simple as tough work schedules, a big presentation, and fights with a partner. Whereas, examples of permanent or chronic stress includes loss of a loved one, traumatic childhood, depression or loneliness, etc.

Whatever it is, it needs to be managed when trying to learn self-discipline in life. Some mental conditioning activities include counselling, yoga, or medications – things we shall discuss in detail in the next chapter.

4. Procrastination

Procrastination is another hindrance in becoming self-disciplined. Procrastination is the practice of delaying things with lame excuses. We all do it, intentionally and sometimes unintentionally. It is the evil root cause of wasting time till the eleventh hour and then doing things in a hasty manner. You must realize that there is no time like now and if you aren't making the most of it and utilizing the available resources, you are going to fail in achieving your goals. The key is to work on today so that your tomorrows are successful and fulfilling.

5. False Hope Syndrome

False hope syndrome is synonymous to having too high of expectations. When expectations are too unrealistic and you fail to accomplish your desired goals, you are bound to feel bad and want to give up. Like stated several times, things need time, energy, and stability. When there is a wide gap between the expectations you have and expectations you should have, problems will propagate automatically.

Summary Conclusion

Distraction, concentration, attention, and focus are all products of the mind and can be influenced by your thoughts. So how important is it to control your thoughts and direct them to a worth goal or outcome you desire..

How do we think? You would think that with all the progress in science, technology, and psychology, an answer would be readily available for this question. The images, sounds and smells that we can conjure at will, how are they formed in our brains? Though theories have been postulated, the puzzle is still, mostly, unsolved. It is even considered unsolvable by some, but the same has been said of many discoveries and innovations on the world of science. It is known that we think in two ways; visually and verbally. This means that you might picture a place or person in your head while thinking of them, or you might simply verbalize a description of the object of your thoughts. This may depend on your proximity to that place or person, or how well you know them. Although, it doesn't do much to answer such questions as what exactly is happening in our brains when we think? It shows that we are well on our way to demystifying this concept.

For now, we can tell for certain that, unlike what pop culture would have you believe, we utilize a much higher percentage of our brains than a puny 10%. And how could we not?

Place electrodes on a person's head, ask them to think a variety of thoughts, and you would notice how several spots on their brains light up on a Magnetic Resonance Imaging machine (MRI). It is possible to see areas of the visual cortex show increased activity at the sight of an object or to measure the electrical impulses that are discharged by the pre-frontal cortex when trying to solve a math problem.

Some scientists have also been able to identify neurons as the cells which allow thought. Working at speeds above 100 miles every hour, these neurons transmit electrical signals to each other through their tentacle-like appendages called dendrites. Between the dendrite of two or more neurons are synapses; a gap through which flows the electrical signals that allow us to see, smell or solve things in our minds. The brain, truly, is awe-inspiring for its complexities and many functions, but it must be commanded by you through the use of repetitive thought habits, visualization, meditation etc.

The End